I0470932

Effective Business Communication

By Inklyo.com

Print Edition

ISBN: 1492338656
ISBN-13: 978-1492338659

CONTENTS

1   Introduction   1

2   Listening   7

3   Candor   18

4   Tone   25

5   Simplicity   34

6   Consistency   41

7   Conclusion   48

8   Acknowledgments and Works Cited   52

INTRODUCTION

"Your ability to convey your ideas to others will be an enormous determinant to your success."

– Warren Buffett

From the moment we're born, we're constantly communicating, broadcasting our needs, wants, and thoughts to the world around us. But don't let that ubiquitous nature fool you. Communicating well is hard work, and not doing so can have disastrous results. This is never more true than in business, where miscommunication can lead to strained working relationships, missed sales opportunities, loss of revenue, and even total business meltdowns. Failure to communicate— properly, clearly, in a timely manner, or at all—is at the heart of most business failures, maybe even all, if you look closely enough.

That is where this book comes in. Drawing on the knowledge of top business leaders and communicators, this book will teach you the five fundamentals of communication that will help you succeed at work— whether you are an entry-level employee or a CEO. This knowledge will enable you to overcome the most common communication errors that lead to business failure. Because written communication can be one of hardest ways to express your thoughts and ideas, each chapter will end with practical tips to help you apply these fundamentals to your writing. Given that the person reading your written communication doesn't receive the cues we rely on to express our intent during in-person communication, such as body language, tone of voice, and facial expression, it's no wonder it's so easy to go astray.

But before we can get there, we must first review the basics of communication and explore why good communication is the key to business success.

Back to basics

The simplest definition of communication is a message that is sent between two parties: the sender and the receiver. That's it! It's one person telling another person something: a baby crying because she's hungry; a customer calling because he didn't receive his order; a coworker sending a meeting request; a smile, a frown, or a laugh. Communication is at the heart of every human interaction, even those without words. And what is the main goal of all this communication? To understand and be understood. We do this in several different ways:

1. Writing

2. Reading

3. Speaking

4. Listening

5. Acting

6. Observing

You'll want to note that only two of the six means of communication involve using your own words. It is easy to forget how much more there is to communication beyond speaking and writing. Your words do matter, but there's more to communication than just what you say, especially at work. The five skills discussed in this book apply to each method of communication. Mastering them will enable you to communicate effectively and efficiently while avoiding the common pitfalls that lead to failure.

In business, there are two types of communication: internal and external. Internal communication is all the communication that happens within an organization—memos, policies, guidebooks, reports, and emails between coworkers. External communication is all the communication that occurs between an organization and the public. This can be anything from ads, press releases, and web site content to phone calls from customers. It is easy to assume that external communication has more value to a company than internal communication does, because, well, customers are the ones with the money. But developing relationships with coworkers—your peers, superiors, and subordinates—is incredibly important, perhaps even the most important thing you'll do at work, and this is completely dependent on your communication skills. Failing to cultivate good relationships with those you work with, work for, or manage will make success an uphill battle. An organization with excellent internal communication will run smoothly, allowing its members to progress toward a mutual goal, which will ultimately affect the quality of external communication. As Warren Buffett, CEO of Berkshire Hathaway, says in the quote at the beginning of this chapter, the ability to communicate well is a huge factor in business success—both individually and organizationally.

So what can happen to a business when communication fails? The consequences can go far beyond losing a customer or receiving a little bad publicity. Business failures related to communication can lead to a product flopping, devastate a business, and even cause loss of life. Let's examine a few real-life examples of such failures.

BP Oil Spill: On April 20, 2010, an explosion occurred on Deepwater Horizon, a drilling rig operated by BP. The rig sank and thousands of gallons of oil spilled into the Gulf of Mexico. The 2010 BP oil spill has been attributed in part to the company's failure to communicate risks.

BP has been accused of failing to ensure that important information was given to those who needed it. For example, while the captains on the rig were responsible for both environmental concerns and the crew's safety, they were left out of decisions dealing with drilling operations and potential risks. The company's onshore location also could not monitor data from the offshore location in real time. The company also appears to have had no process in place to ensure that the parties overseeing the operation could directly communicate. Ultimately, the problem was that the right information was not given to the right people, partially because no good communication processes were in place. These communication failures led to the largest offshore oil spill in US history, causing the deaths of 11 workers and devastating the local environment.

Cartoon Network Bomb Scare: In 2007, the Cartoon Network undertook a guerrilla marketing campaign to promote its movie, *Aqua Teen Hunger Force Colon Movie Film for Theaters*, which is based on one of its shows. As part of the campaign, the company secretly placed LED signs featuring one of the movie's characters in train stations, overpasses, and other high visibility areas around Boston. Unfortunately for the Cartoon Network, the devices, which included visible wires and batteries taped to the bottom of the signs, looked similar to homemade bombs and they were reported to the authorities by frightened members of the public. This led to the dispatch of the Boston Police Department bomb squad and the shutting down over a dozen highways and transit stations across the city. Several people were briefly arrested in connection with the event and faced charges of placing a hoax device that caused panic. Such a reaction could have easily been avoided, but the company failed to secure permits or communicate its marketing plan to authorities. While fans of the show mocked the reaction, the mistake was a costly one: the company had to pay $2 million—the cost the city incurred because of the incident—as part of a legal settlement. *Jim Samples,* the manager of the Cartoon Network, resigned after twelve years with the company to avoid criminal charges.

BlackBerry PlayBook: When BlackBerry introduced the PlayBook, the company's version of the iPad, in 2010, it failed monumentally in communicating its product to consumers. In a technical sense, the PlayBook outperformed in the iPad in almost every aspect, but this fact was lost in the complicated, dry message of Jim Balsillie, the company's co-CEO. While Apple's Steve Jobs used simple, straightforward words *to* describe the iPad and its features, referring to it as "so much more intimate than a laptop and so much more capable than a smartphone with [its] gorgeous, large display," Balsillie's message was almost indecipherable: "And that's sort of an obvious thing, but also there's tremendous architectural contention at play. And so I'm going to really frame our mobile architectural distinction. We've taken two fundamentally different approaches in their causalness. It's a causal difference, not just nuance. It's not just a causal direction that I'm going to really articulate here—and feel free to go as deep as you want—it's really as fundamental as causalness." (What?) That the PlayBook specs were better didn't matter when the public didn't get the message; at its official launch, co-CEO Mike Lazaridis didn't even demonstrate the PlayBook's functions! As of the second quarter of 2011, the PlayBook's tablet market share was only 3.3%, compared to the iPad's 61.3%.

These examples demonstrate a range of communication failures and outcomes. When a company doesn't properly communicate the benefits of its product, it will never beat its competitors, and if a company doesn't clearly communicate risks to its employees, it endangers their lives. A misunderstanding between employees due to a poorly worded email is unlikely to have such disastrous effects, but it can still lead to strained relationships or even disciplinary action, depending on what was said. Big or small, most communication failures are caused by a few common factors:

1. Not listening

2. Withholding information

3. Complex messages

4. Vague messages

5. Ineffective communication processes

Whether you are struggling with communication failures or just want to improve your ability to communicate in general, there are several *fundamentals* of good business communication that can help:

1. Listening

2. Candor

3. Simplicity

4. Tone

5. Consistency

We'll cover these skills in the rest of the book. For each fundamental, we'll examine what successful business leaders and communicators, including Jack Welch, Sheryl Sandberg, and Seth Godin, have said about them. We'll examine why they're necessary and how you can apply them in your work life.

Let's get started.

LISTENING

"Listening and picking up on subtext are at least as important to building emotional connections as anything you say."

– Arlene Dickinson

The first step in effective communication is listening. It is impossible to have truly successful communication without listening—listening to those above you, to those below you, to your peers, and to your customers and clients. When communicating with others, we often get caught up in our own desire to express our thoughts, ideas, and feelings. However, as Arlene Dickinson, CEO of Venture Communications and judge on Canada's *Dragons' Den*, says in the quote above, listening is as important as anything we say. This is especially true in business, where effective listening can lead to increased productivity, higher quality of work, greater customer satisfaction, better work relationships, and improved morale. When you are listened to, you feel appreciated and motivated; when you listen, you discover what you need to be successful in any interaction.

The stages and types of listening

No matter the form it takes, communication requires a sender and a receiver, the receiver being, obviously, the listener. Receivers can use several different methods of listening when receiving and processing a message, but let's start by going over the stages of listening. You might be thinking that you already know how to listen, but understanding what is going on behind this mostly automatic process will help you improve this skill.

The listening process has five stages: receiving, understanding, remembering, evaluating, and responding. To keep this short, we can combine the middle three stages into one simple step, since they are related to the same thing—processing.

1. Receiving: In this stage, you are taking in the message from the speaker. You do this by hearing what is being said and how it is being said. This includes listening to the speaker is saying and watching for nonverbal clues.

2. Processing: In the processing stage of listening, you're internally evaluating the message. You are analyzing what was said and attempting to find its meaning. You are interpreting the words used and the tone of voice in which they were said and evaluating body language and other nonverbal clues.

3. Responding: This stage is when you become the speaker. You respond to the speaker verbally and nonverbally. In this stage, you should be acknowledging that you received and understood the speaker's message.

We listen in several different ways, and while we each may use one type more than others, most people use each type of listening at least sometimes. The problem is that not all types are created equal!

Selective listening

When you listen selectively, you are hearing only what you want to hear. Sometimes this is intentional, perhaps because you don't want to hear what is being said, but sometimes it occurs when you aren't giving the speaker your full attention. Imagine this situation: You are telling a coworker about a presentation you gave to a client the previous week. Your coworker is looking at some papers on her desk and not really responding. Before you are able to ask for her help in planning the logistics of the new deal, she interrupts to tell you about this great opportunity she has coming up. How do you feel? Probably annoyed she wasn't really listening and made the conversation all about her.

We all do this occasionally. Someone says something that reminds us about an issue we wanted to discuss with them, and we can't help interrupting. Sometimes we listen selectively because of the person doing the speaking—maybe it's someone we know who is overly chatty or we don't like that much. The problem is that selective listening causes us to miss the message or only hear part of it. This can lead to confusion, assumptions, or overreactions. To avoid selective listening, listen actively (more on that soon) and make it point not to cut people off.

Passive listening

Passive listening takes almost no effort because the listener is essentially not responding at all to what is being said. The listener is generally responding with some form of nonverbal communication but adds little or nothing to the conversation, except maybe an occasional "Mm hmm." We've all been on both sides of this type of listening. Your coworker is blathering on about how his car broke down over the weekend and his husband was out of town so he had to get a loaner and then the rental place tried to give him a stick shift car but he can't drive standard so . . . Meanwhile, you've checked out and are planning a response to a pressing email, or maybe you're thinking about what you want for lunch. Whatever the case, you aren't really hearing what is being said. Perhaps you're talking to your manager about an upcoming meeting. She's got a blank look on her face and is nodding from time to time, but not even in the right places. That's passive listening. The problem with this type of listening is obvious: the message isn't being received and relationships may be strained or damaged as a result.

Fixing passive listening is pretty easy. When someone is speaking, give your full attention. If your coworker is giving you a blow-by-blow of his weekend woes and you are really busy, ask if you can talk later, or listen actively for a few minutes before telling him you need to get back to work. If your manager's eyes are glazing over while you speak, ensure you're being to the point, or if necessary, ask if there is a better time for you two to talk.

Attentive listening

Attentive listening has some great, positive aspects. It involves being engaged in a speaker's words and offering verbal and nonverbal feedback. An attentive listener may ask questions to get more information from the speaker and will use appropriate and sincere body language to indicate interest and understanding. You probably noticed, however, that I said attentive listening has *some* positive aspects, so you may be wondering what's wrong with attentive listening. Well, nothing exactly, but it is very fact based and thus can lack an understanding of the speaker's emotions. Sometimes, this kind of listening is all that is needed; for example, maybe your subordinate wants to schedule a meeting with you, so you ask her what time she was considering. That's really all that is needed in that conversation. She sent a message and you received it.

When a message deals with emotions, however, and you are only listening for the facts, you fail to get the whole meaning. Again, the way to fill this gap in this type of listening is through active listening, so let's cover that.

Active listening

Active listening uses the positive aspect of attentive listening—listening for the facts—but also involves listening for emotions and feelings, allowing you to capture the whole message. When you are actively listening, you are being patient and understanding, you are showing the speaker that you care about what he is saying, and you are acknowledging the feelings behind what is being said. Imagine that you approach your boss with a problem and he takes a few minutes to listen to you fully. He makes steady eye contact, encourages you to continue speaking, asks relevant questions to gain more information or to increase clarity, and acknowledges your feelings about the issue. How do you feel? Listened to and understood! Active listening is very similar to a concept called empathetic listening, which we'll go over in detail next, followed by practical tips to help you use empathetic listening in your daily work life and writing.

"Seek first to understand, then be understood."

– Stephen Covey

The quote used to start this section is Habit 5 of Stephen Covey's *The 7 Habits of Highly Effective People*. As Covey points out in his book, we spend years learning how to speak, read, and write, but very little time, if any, is spent teaching us to listen effectively. Listening to understand, says Covey, is extremely important, but most of us listen with the intent to reply. As we discussed above, how often are you listening to someone speak but already planning what you want to say next? How much of what someone is saying to you are you really hearing? We often assume we know what a speaker is saying to us, so we miss what is really being said. Listening in this way is at the heart of many misunderstandings, and listening effectively and empathetically is the only solution.

Empathetic listening

To first understand, Covey recommends a technique he calls "empathetic listening." We must consciously seek to understand the speaker and her frame of reference, not focus on our own thoughts, beliefs, and histories or choosing what to say next when listening to someone speak (thus choosing to be understood first). Empathetic listening is listening without judgment and listening for what the speaker is feeling and doing, not just saying. Often, a speaker's true meaning is hidden under the words she is using—perhaps due to fear, pride, embarrassment, and so on. For most of us, listening in this way is quite different from what we would usually do.

Empathetic listening does not involve refuting, advising, agreeing/disagreeing, or attempting to resolve the speaker's problem. It is simply listening to understand. You might be wondering how this type of listening applies to business. It is an excellent way to improve working relationships, to build trust with employees or clients, or to discern what someone needs or expects from you.

Here's how you do it: When someone speaks to you, give her your full attention. Don't plan what you'll say next. Just listen, and absolutely do not interrupt. When she has finished speaking, repeat back what she has said. You needn't do this verbatim. In fact, this can seem insincere; instead, summarize what has been said and the emotions you perceive behind it:

Coworker: This project is driving me crazy! The deadline is ridiculous!

You: You seem like you're feeling really stressed out about the project and are worried about missing your deadline.

This might seem silly or awkward to you, and your natural inclination might be to offer advice ("When I am really stressing about a deadline, I . . ." or "You should ask if you can work overtime to get your project done on time"), but just let the person know you have heard and understood what she is saying. Here are a few other ways you could start your reply:

1. If I am understanding you . . .

2. You feel . . .

3. What I am hearing is . . . Is that right?

At this point, your coworker may further explain how stressed she is feeling, which may lead her to her own solution, or she may ask for your advice. If you still aren't at the heart of what your coworker is trying to convey, you can continue to use empathetic listening skills to get there. Continue to paraphrase what your coworker is telling you, and ask open-ended questions (questions that require more than a yes or no answer) to get more information. Sometimes conversations in which you use empathetic listening may seem to take longer than conversations in which you're listening as usual. This may be true, but the payoff is in the understanding you gain, which will ultimately save you time and effort.

Writing tips

It may not be immediately obvious how you can apply listening to your written communication, but there are a few things to be learned here.

Determine your audience. Before you can write effectively, you should consider your readers. The tone of your writing and the language you use will vary considerably depending on your audience—think of how differently you would give a presentation to the CEO of your company versus a presentation to a potential client. Before you start writing, gather as much information as possible about your audience. If you are replying to an email from a single person, this is quite easy. If you will be writing something for a larger audience, you need to think about who they are, why they're reading what you are writing, when they'll be reading it, how they'll be reading it, and how much of the topic they understand. Consider whether a second audience will be reading your correspondence and determine whether there is anything they'll need to know (perhaps some background information or the definition of a term) or even if there is something they shouldn't know.

Let's say that you are writing a report on next year's projected sales for the department heads. After they view it, however, it will be presented to the sales people from the satellite offices when they visit company headquarters for the annual sales meeting. Unfortunately, sales projections aren't looking good:

Projected sales for FY2013 are down 30% from where they were this time last year. I recommend that we close the five satellite offices with the lowest sales in FY2012.

This would be fine if your report were simply going to the department heads, but can you imagine the panic this would create at the annual sales meeting among those from the satellite offices? What might happen if another audience, like shareholders, were to read the report after it's presented at the sales meeting? Always consider your audience and be sure to determine whether there will be a second or even a third audience.

Don't skim correspondence. If you are writing a reply to someone, be sure that you really read what has been sent to you. Much like selective listening, skimming an email or letter can cause you to miss important information. This may include instructions you may have received from your boss or a specific request from a client. Ensure that you thoroughly understand what they want from you before you begin so that you don't omit something. Being on the receiving end of this situation is especially frustrating for customers, who are often already agitated by the time they reach out to a company. Taking time to understand correspondence fully will save you both time and frustration in the long run.

Imagine that you receive the following email from a customer:

To whom it may concern,

I am writing regarding an issue I am having with a gift certificate for Super Music Warehouse that I purchased from your company on May 13, 2012. The store went out of business before I could redeem it, so I would like a refund. Actually, if it was possible to exchange it for a different one, that would be my preference, but if it's not, a refund is fine.

Sincerely,

Jill Smith

It's a busy day. The phones are ringing non-stop, you've got a bunch of other customer emails to respond to, and so you skim. You see "refund," "store went out of business" and nothing else. The customer wants a refund for a valid reason? No problem! You shoot off this email:

Ms. Smith,

I'm sorry to hear about the problems you've had redeeming your gift certificate. Your credit card has been refunded the full amount of $50. Please allow up to 10 business days for this to be reflected in your account.

Best,

Jane

Now, this response is okay. Jill might be happy enough, though she might be confused or frustrated that you didn't fully respond to her issue. Worse, your company lost a sale. The following email would have better addressed the customer's needs, making her more likely to purchase from you again, and it would've better benefited your company's bottom line:

Ms. Smith,

I'm sorry to hear about the problems you've had redeeming your gift certificate. It wouldn't be a problem at all for you to exchange the gift certificate for another of your choosing. I've credited your account for $50. You can redeem this on our website (www.giftcertificatesforyou.com) or by phone at 1-800-111-1111.

Best,

Jane

If for some reason an exchange was not possible, it would've been better to add a line to the first email explaining this so that Jill would feel validated that her complaint was heard and that her issue was addressed fully.

Write empathetically. You can absolutely use the principle behind empathetic listening in your written correspondence. This is especially effective when responding to complaints or concerns. Take the time to seek more information when necessary and to acknowledge the sender's feelings. Business communication is often so fact based and results driven that we forget the need to be empathetic. Writing empathetically starts small: Refer to your addressees by name. Addressing someone personally is the first step in making them feel you're listening to them and their concerns. Next, validate what they've said to you, and then address the main concern or topic of their correspondence.

For example, if one of your employees has emailed you about a problem he's having with another coworker, try asking him for his opinion on what should be done rather getting angry or forcing a solution.

Hi Matt,

This is a little hard for me to bring up, as I don't want to ruffle any feathers, but I'm just not sure what to do anymore. I've been having some problems with Susan lately. As you know, our quarters are quite tight. A few weeks ago, Susan started listening to the radio all day. I just can't concentrate when music is playing. Sometimes it makes having phone conversations difficult. I don't want to cause a rift between Susan and me, so I'm hoping you can help.

Thanks,

Dave

Maybe you're busy or feel Dave is being silly over the whole thing, but don't respond with this:

I don't have time for this. Tell her to turn it off, or just deal with it.

Go for something more empathetic, and you'll take care of the problem sooner, because without action, this isn't going to go away. You'll only hear about it again. Ensure there are no hard feelings all around, and your employees will also know they can come to you:

Dave,

It sounds like the music is making it hard for you to work, but you aren't sure how best to approach Susan about it. Can you think of any solutions that might work for both of you?

Regards,

Matt

Here, you've shown Dave that you heard what he had to say, and you've provided gentle guidance toward resolving the issue.

CANDOR

"Lack of candor basically blocks smart ideas, fast action, and good people contributing all the stuff they've got. It's a killer."

– Jack Welch

Jack Welch, former CEO of General Electric, is well known as being a proponent of candor in business communications. In his book, *Winning*, Welch specifically addresses the lack of candor and honesty in performance reviews:

"I always end up asking audiences for a show of hands to the question 'How many of you have received an honest, straight-between-the-eyes-feedback session in the last year, where you came out knowing exactly what you have to do to improve and where you stand in the organization?' On a good day, I get 20 percent of the hands up. Most of the time, it is closer to 10 percent."

Although it is important for leaders to receive honest feedback (something we'll discuss later), it is imperative that they also provide employees with regular, candid, and honest feedback and performance appraisals. People can change much more easily if they know what is expected of them and how to improve. Your employees will work harder and do better work if you give them the opportunity. The problem, of course, is that this is easier said than done. We're socialized to be polite to others, so speaking honestly, particularly about performance issues, can feel like going against everything you were taught about speaking to others. Or maybe you don't mind telling it like it is, but your bluntness makes people defensive. Regardless, being candid doesn't have to be an all-or-nothing deal. You can find a happy medium between being rude and dishonest with your employees. If you aren't a leader (yet!), don't skip this chapter; you can apply these same tips in any difficult interaction you may need to have with your coworkers.

First, know your audience. Are you doing a review or addressing an issue with an employee you know to be sensitive or defensive? You need to take that into consideration even if that type of personality is different from yours. You can't expect someone else to react exactly as you would. If this person prefers communication to be blunt and to the point, you can adjust what you're going to say to suit. Next, find time when you can speak with this person privately; in front of others, and especially in meetings, is absolutely not the time to give this kind of feedback.

When you discuss an issue with an employee, try using "I" statements, such as "I noticed there were some errors in the data in your last order request," rather than "You" statements, such as "You made a lot of mistakes in your last order request." While both sentences are saying the same thing, the "I" statement depersonalizes what is said a little, which keeps your employee from feeling defensive or under attack. Now that you have highlighted the issue, explain to the employee the results of such a mistake. For example, "The data errors led us to ship the wrong number of units to our client, who was very unhappy." This should help the employee understand the gravity of the situation, and it sets both of you up for the final remark—explaining what should be done to remedy the issue. To put it all together: "I noticed there were some errors in the data in your last order request. That led us to ship the wrong number of units to our client, who was very unhappy. In the future, I need you to double check the numbers before turning order requests in."

If you are addressing an ongoing problem, particularly one you've addressed in the past, you may need to add a little here. Besides telling the employee what you expect him to change, tell him how you'll be judging that change and what will happen if he fails to make the requested improvement. For example, "We've discussed the need for you to verify the data before turning in orders, but unfortunately there have been errors again twice this month. Going forward, after you check your numbers, I need you to send your orders to me first so that I can go over them before sending them to shipping. If I continue to find errors, I will have to take you off the account."

If this is a performance review, rather than addressing a single issue on the fly, you can continue in this way with any other issues that need discussing, but try sandwiching negative remarks with genuine positive ones. Start with the good and end with the good. If you have time, add some in the middle too. This will help keep your employee from feeling discouraged or attacked while still allowing you to be candid. Do note that you shouldn't save criticisms for performance reviews. If an employee is doing something that needs changing and her yearly review is seven months away, don't wait! Tell her now and give her a chance to succeed. Nothing is as demoralizing and humiliating as going into a performance review—where you are already nervous but maybe a bit hopeful—and hearing that your boss thinks you have been doing something wrong for months when you were under the impression that things were fine.

Perhaps the most important thing you can do as a leader if you want to be candid with your employees is to remember that they can't read your mind. Giving them candid feedback starts with you setting clear expectations and goals.

"Speak as well as seek the truth."

– Sheryl Sandberg

What Sheryl Sandberg, COO of Facebook, means is that it is as important for everyone, especially those in charge, to seek candidness as it is to be candid. We've already discussed being candid in our communication with others, but here we're going to talk about why we want others to be candid with us.

In her speech to the 2012 graduating class of Harvard Business School, Sandberg noted how difficult it is for managers and those in charge to get honest feedback and opinions from their employees:

"All of us, and especially leaders, need to speak and hear the truth. The workplace is an especially difficult place for anyone to tell the truth, because no matter how flat we want our organizations to be, all organizations have some form of hierarchy. What that means is that one person's performance is assessed by someone else's perception. This is not a setup for honesty."

She noted later that it can be almost impossible for leaders to get honest feedback no matter how many times they ask their employees for it. This makes sense. Employees may fear offending others, how they'll be perceived, or whether their feedback will come up negatively in a later performance review. Basically, they don't want to get fired. To quell such fears and encourage honesty, Sandberg suggests that leaders be honest with their employees about their own faults, which gives their employees permission to agree with them, rather than trying to point out these faults on their own. For example, if you're a department manager and you know you have a tendency to micromanage, mention that occasionally when meeting with your employees. This may make them comfortable enough to mention something that has been bothering them or something they think could help the department.

It is important to note what happens in a workplace where good, open feedback is not encouraged or well received: things fail, deadlines run late, clients are lost, and productivity and morale go down. What do your employees tell you in this sort of climate? They tell you only what they think you want to hear, even if it isn't what you need to hear. They say yes, when the answer should be no. So what can you do?

The first thing you need to do is to take any honest feedback you receive calmly and with an open mind. If you've been angry about your employees' past comments, stop reacting this way. Don't take anything personally, even if it is personal. It's all business, and that's how you should view it. If you listen to your employees, you can improve yourself, them, and ultimately, the business.

You may need to reassure employees that they won't get in trouble for being candid with you, which is especially true if you've reacted poorly to past feedback. Try Sandberg's tactic above to start actively seeking and receiving what you need to hear.

You can't just seek feedback—you have to use it! Of course, not everything you get from your employees will be actionable or even good, but if you're listening with an open mind and a willingness to change, you'll find plenty of excellent ideas and opportunities. If your employees are telling you that one of your ideas stinks, hear them out and ask them how they think it can be improved. You hired them, so they must be smart, creative, and talented, right?

Acknowledge and appreciate the feedback you receive, even if you won't act on it. This will help further reassure employees that what they've said was heard (going back to our chapter on listening) and welcomed, and it will encourage them to continue being candid with you.

Writing tips

It is just as important to be candid in your written communication as it is when speaking. But it can be trickier because it is easier to come across as rude or blunt in writing since your body language or tone of voice can't make your intent obvious.

Practice clarity. When you are trying to write candidly, it is incredibly important to be as clear as possible. Don't beat around the bush or use overly flowery language, and don't hide your point under jargon or rambling anecdotes. Make your point understood by using common words and avoid using too many acronyms—when your writing is full of acronyms, your readers often must backtrack to find their meaning. This tip is particularly important when writing for clients, customers, or basically anyone outside your organization who may not understand its terminology or jargon.

Imagine you are writing to a potential client, and you'd like her to consider selling your new camera in her small chain of electronics stores. She has no knowledge of your company, and you are unsure about her level of expertise regarding photography. Don't write:

The TTL metering of the new SNP3556 is unparalleled at current.

Instead, try writing something that anyone would understand, no matter their level of knowledge about cameras:

Our newest camera, the Snappy 3556, is the best in its class. It is capable of measuring light levels through its lens, rather than a separate metering window, which allows users to control the amount of light emitted by the flash.

Don't omit. Part of being candid is being honest, so don't omit or withhold important information. Be sure to include all the facts your reader needs to understand the point you are making. This will help to keep them from getting defensive or argumentative and allow them to make the best possible decisions or take the most suitable action. Consider this: the American Management Association's *Global Study of Current Trends and Future Possibilities 2007-2017* found that "High-performance organizations understand the power of good communication and of sharing information. Information is viewed as something to be shared rather than something to be hoarded for the purpose of power and control."

Be polite. Communication in the business world often occurs only through writing; depending on your field, this may involve critiquing someone's work or ideas—a touchy subject for many! Whether you are editing a coworker's report or responding to a client's proposal, one way you can try to convey your intent is to always be as polite as you can. Use "Please" and "Thank you" whenever possible, and make suggestions rather than demands. Doing so allows you to be honest without offending.

For example, if one of your coworkers has asked you to go over a report for him before he sends it off to the boss, and you're coming across a lot of sentences you don't understand, don't leave a comment saying this:

I can't understand what you're talking about here! It makes absolutely no sense! You need to fix this.

No matter how you really mean it, this can come across the wrong way. Try this simple change instead:

The meaning here isn't really clear. Please revise this sentence.

This uses polite language and frames the issue as being a problem with the language, not the writer, and will be much better received than the first example.

TONE

"When dealing with people, let us remember we are not dealing with creatures of logic. We are dealing with creatures of emotion, creatures bristling with prejudices and motivated by pride and vanity."

– Dale Carnegie

Now that we've talked about being candid, we should probably talk about tone. What you say is important, but how you say it will completely affect how it is received. As we discussed, being candid can do great things for you in the business world, but if your candidness is perceived as mean, you can probably expect to receive defensiveness, negative reactions, and poor outcomes in return, regardless of where you fall in the chain of command.

This problem mainly arises when candor is perceived as criticism. "Wait," you may be thinking, "wasn't I just told that I should be honest and open and provide candid feedback?" Well, yes, but that's not what we're talking about here. Being candid doesn't mean finding fault or criticizing others for the sake of honesty. No one likes to be criticized and criticism is rarely received well. In the classic *How to Win Friends and Influence People*, Dale Carnegie discusses at length why criticism does not work—in fact, it's the very first principle in the book. Carnegie says, "Criticism is futile because it puts a person on the defensive and usually makes him strive to justify himself. Criticism is dangerous, because it wounds a person's precious pride, hurts his sense of importance, and arouses resentment . . . The resentment that criticism engenders can demoralize employees, family members and friends, and still not correct the situation that has been condemned."

The tone you use when being candid can make the difference between being seen as providing necessary or needed feedback and being seen as being unnecessarily critical. If you are consistently talking to your employees or coworkers in a way that is perceived as critical or rude, they will shut down on you. Your valid points will be perceived as invalid, and their motivation to do well will drop. This is human nature. Being critical, rude, or outright mean will not get you the results you want, even if you think people need to take your comments "less personally."

If you know you have a tendency toward criticism or you struggle with keeping your tone appropriate, you may first need to stop approaching situations or certain people in an immediately negative way. We've all worked with or for someone like this—that person who is angry or negative before words are even spoken, no matter the intended topic. If this is you, it's important to realize you can't have any sort of effective communication this way. It may help to take a minute in such situations and ask yourself whether you want to be right at that moment or successful in the long term.

Being mindful of your tone isn't about sugarcoating things or even about being liked by your coworkers. Using a respectful tone and approaching situations consciously will make you more successful in all aspects of your business life. If you need more convincing, look at it this way: Why waste 20 minutes criticizing one of your employees about work you consider substandard when you can have a 10-minute conversation respectfully discussing your expectations and how that employee can improve her work? If you go the criticism route, you can likely expect to repeat the process in a few months because your aggressive approach caused your employee to go on the defensive and ignore your valid points. Or maybe you'll spend weeks searching for and training a new employee because the one you were aggressive with was tired of being perceived as a bad worker. Maybe she was, but maybe you lost someone who could have done excellent work for you, if only you'd given her what she needed to succeed.

When your tone is angry or critical, people feel unappreciated, bullied. They may feel you are setting them up for failure because they don't feel like what you are saying to them is valuable or reasonable. Learning the difference between the various types of communicating can help you avoid these pitfalls.

"I start with the notion that if there is something that's broken, I can fix it. So there's no reason to get mad at somebody. I'm always starting with a certain amount of trust for anybody I'm dealing with. And by the way, even if you do get angry, it's not going to solve the problem. All it's going to do is reverberate around the office that so and so made a mistake and so and so is angry at them. Then a whole cloud of frustrations and anger pervades the office. And so all of a sudden you get a breakdown in the culture of cooperation and collegiality, and the common mission goes out the window. And it'll take you a week or so to get everybody back together."

– Robert L. Johnson

Robert L. Johnson, founder of Black Entertainment Television, is right in the quote above. Anger is a pervasive emotion, spreading through the workplace and causing malcontent. If some consider you angry, critical, or negative, that image of you spreads too; more people take notice than you may realize, and people may be reluctant to work for or with you. If you're the CEO or the owner, this matters doubly because it all starts with you—and remember, your company's reputation will spread among both potential employees and potential clients.

Of course, work must get done, and there are times when conversations must take place, so let's examine the different types of communicating to determine how assertive communication can improve the tone you use when communicating, which will in turn improve relationships across the workplace.

Communication can generally be divided into four basic types: passive, aggressive, passive-aggressive, and assertive. Most people use a combination of these types of communicating, so you will likely recognize a little bit of yourself in each type—both your good and bad traits. Identifying the areas in which you'd like to change will go a long way in improving your working and business relationships.

Passive communication is communicating without expressing needs, rights, or desires. A passive communicator tries to avoid confrontation and will concede or give up quickly and easily when challenged. He is often much more concerned with what someone thinks of him than about communicating his point effectively, and he may use indirect language to express his thoughts or feelings. He may also be dishonest or blame others, or he may complain to someone else rather than address the person who needs to hear the complaint. He will often appear submissive and may fidget, avoid eye contact, or speak quietly or in an uncertain voice.

Aggressive communication is communicating in a way that is critical and blaming of others. An aggressive communicator isn't interested in hearing what others have to say; she only cares about getting what she wants. She may threaten, intimidate, or pressure others and may use sarcasm to win arguments. An aggressive communicator takes an authoritarian approach to things, is likely to interrupt when others are speaking, and escalates situations or discussions into arguments. She may yell or use an unnecessarily loud voice, and she may even resort to profanity or name calling.

Passive-aggressive communication combines the traits of passive and aggressive communicating. It is hostile and aggressive, but in a way that is subtle and indirect. Of all the types, it is the most manipulative. Rather than speaking with someone about his issue, the passive-aggressive communicator may work to "get even" in subtle ways, which may include giving the cold shoulder to the person with whom he is upset, conveniently "forgetting" to convey important information, sabotaging that person's work or performance, or even simply procrastinating. He may gossip or make catty or cutting remarks, give indirect or clipped responses, sigh or roll his eyes when speaking, or make impatient or angry facial expressions that contradict his words. Picture when someone says "It's fine" in a way that makes it perfectly clear that things are not fine.

Assertive communication is communicating directly and with confidence, positivity, and respect. An assertive communicator expresses her needs, feelings, and thoughts; she takes personal accountability for her actions and can defend her rights while respecting others. She actively listens and seeks to understand those with whom she is speaking, is direct without being hostile or abrupt, and attempts to solve problems. An assertive communicator uses body language that matches her message, makes good eye contact, and speaks in a steady, calm tone.

While there is often a time when a passive or aggressive way of communicating is necessary, you want to aim for assertive communicating whenever possible. Try the following tips to add assertiveness to your communications:

Be confident. If you aren't confident in yourself and what you have to say, you'll never achieve assertiveness. Fake it if you must, but be sure to sound confident and like you believe in (and know) what you are talking about.

Take responsibility. Be accountable for your words and actions and their subsequent outcomes. This will increase the respect others have for you, which will increase your perceived authority. When you own your mistakes, you are perceived as honest and trustworthy, so don't blame or point fingers.

Don't take it personally. Whether it's feedback from someone you work for (or someone who works for you) or misplaced anger from a client, don't take it personally. Little of it has to do with who you are as a person and letting yourself get offended will only lead to anger or aggression on your part.

Be aware. Understand how your actions and words affect others and recognize that these have the power to hurt. Not everyone will be able to not take things personally! When you always try to win an argument— or worse, when you try to get revenge—you are creating a negative, hostile image of yourself, and little gets accomplished aside from hard feelings and more work. Be aware also of your responses to the actions and words of others and take time to consider how you should react to achieve the best possible outcome.

Express yourself. Use facts and feelings to explain your perspective. Don't assume everyone knows what you mean and be sure to use many "I" statements to get your point across.

Of course, you can be careful about your tone, practice active listening, and speak using assertive communication yet still encounter defensiveness in others. That's because, as we discussed above, you're dealing with humans who have all kinds of emotions, judgments, and preconceived notions. If you're working toward changing your communication style to something less aggressive and hostile, it may take some time for people to stop responding reactively to you. Luckily, there are a few methods you can use to combat defensiveness and open the lines of communication:

Encourage expression. When you are dealing with someone whom you know is defensive or is becoming defensive, encourage her to express her thoughts or feelings. Ask open-ended questions and, when needed, ask what she is feeling. This will help you understand her perspective, allowing you to respect it even if you disagree.

Seek understanding. This needs to go both ways. Try to make sure you understand what the other person is saying and ensure they understand you. If necessary, ask him to paraphrase your message. You may find that one or both of you is off point or missing something important.

Don't debate. It's hard not to counter every argument with a contrary fact or point, but this will only serve to lengthen the disagreement and encourage defensive behavior. Instead of disagreeing or trying to counter the point, seek to clarify, but only if it actually adds needed information—otherwise, you'll just be perceived as disagreeing.

Stay positive. Try not to get frustrated and be sure to keep your tone positive, rather than angry or aggressive. Stress your positive intentions. As with not debating, staying positive discourages defensiveness because it doesn't give the other person anything else to get upset about, which will allow you to work toward a solution.

Writing tips

Conveying the right tone is especially hard in writing, but it is important if you want your message to be understood. There are a few things you can do to improve the tone of your writing.

Identify your purpose. What are you writing and why? Much like a particular audience will change the way you write, the reason for writing will greatly affect the tone you use. Are you writing a report to present at a conference? Are you writing an email following up on a warm lead? Are you informing? Selling? Take the time to consider what you are trying to accomplish and match your tone to that purpose.

Use personal pronouns. Using personal pronouns makes your tone warmer, more welcoming, and more personal. They enhance the clarity of your message, and they help your reader feel like you are talking directly to them. Personal pronouns also help readers know what applies to them and what applies to you. As discussed before, use "I" statements when giving feedback to avoid sounding critical. If you're speaking as one individual (that is, you are speaking for yourself and not for a group or the organization as a whole), be sure to use "I" instead of "we."

If you are writing an email to an employee about his recent poor sales performance, you could say this:

We recently received the sales figures for Q2, and they are down over 15%, which we were really disappointed about. We need to see this number improve.

The problem is that the tone and language can make the email's desired outcome unclear to the reader. Your employee may wonder whether this was directed at him personally or if this was a department problem, and he may also wonder who "we" refers to—is it just you, or is this also coming from your manager? Try this instead:

I recently received your sales figures for Q2; unfortunately, they are down over 15%. I'm disappointed about this, and I'd like to see this number improve for Q3.

Use positive language. One study found that when we use negative words, stress chemicals are released in our brains, and the person receiving our message experiences increased anxiety and decreased feelings of trust and cooperation. Another study found that if you want your business relationships to flourish, you should make five positive remarks for every one negative remark. So when possible, use positive language to frame your message. Focus on what can be done, rather than what cannot be done. Positive language drives the motivational centers of the brain into action, which is exactly what you want.

Let's continue with our example from the previous tip, but let's add positive language and focus on what else can be done:

Tom,

I wanted to mention how pleased I am about you bringing in the Vandelay account last month. I know it was a lot of work, and you did an excellent job addressing their concerns.

I recently received your sales figures for Q2; unfortunately, they are down over 15%. I'm disappointed about this, and I'd like to see this number improve for Q3. I know you can do this; let's schedule a meeting to discuss strategies to get your numbers back up.

You've conveyed the problem, and you did so by gently framing it with some positive and encouraging words. Tom still knows what is wrong and what he needs to change, but he also knows you aren't angry with him and that you don't think his overall performance is bad. This is going to save him some stress and will make your subsequent meeting easier for both of you. It will also improve your image because employees will see you as encouraging and fair when you take such an approach.

SIMPLICITY

"Simple can be harder than complex: You have to work hard to get your thinking clean to make it simple. But it's worth it in the end because once you get there, you can move mountains."

– Steve Jobs

No one can start a chapter on simplicity better than the late Steve Jobs, co-founder and former CEO of Apple. Jobs was a master of simplicity. He drove himself, those around him, and his company to distill ideas to their most basic element. We touched on this briefly in the introduction—you'll remember the difference between the launches of Apple's iPad and Blackberry's PlayBook. Apple's launch was an excellent example of the Apple way of doing things: determine a need, create a product that fulfills that need and is simple and easy to use, and present the product in a clear, understandable way. This simplicity extends to the shopping experience: Jobs conceptualized the Apple Store as a place where the purchasing experience was as streamlined as its products. With some conscious effort, you can take the clean lines of Apple's products and apply them to your business communications, whether that communication is an advertisement aimed at consumers or a conversation with a coworker.

Antoine de Saint Exupéry, author of *The Little Prince*, said, "It seems that perfection is reached not when there is nothing left to add, but when there is nothing left to take away." Steve Jobs very well could have spoken those words himself. They are similar, albeit much more nicely worded, than the KISS (Keep It Simple, Stupid) principle, which, while originally a design principle, is quite applicable to good communication. To simplify your communication, start by aiming for brevity and conciseness.

Being simple and concise does not mean dumbing down what you are saying. Quite the opposite! When you are communicating simply and concisely, you are deleting all unnecessary information and getting to the essence of what you're attempting to say; everything you're communicating is then important and exactly what your audience needs to understand you. As Einstein said, "Everything should be made as simple as possible, but not simpler." Let's review some strategies for communicating more concisely.

1. Use fewer words.

2. That's all.

Just kidding! There are a few ways you can bring simplicity and brevity into your business communication:

Before you begin, really determine what it is you're trying to say. If you don't fully understand your own point or idea, you'll never communicate it clearly and concisely. When you're planning a presentation or creating marketing materials, there is plenty of time to consider this. In a conversation on the fly, or in a situation such as an interview, this is harder, but is still possible. Take your time, and think before you speak. In such situations, it is perfectly okay to request a moment to think or ask if you can return to a topic.

Once you've determined what you want to say, begin your communication with your main idea or point. Keep it simple and direct. This is where you should use de Saint Exupéry's advice: When discussing

INKLYO.COM

your main idea, distill it to its essence. A big part of communicating with simplicity is to practice candor, which we've already discussed, and to be as precise as possible. If it helps, consider the who, what, where, when, and why of what you want to say.

After you have communicated your main point, follow it with support. However, don't use this as an excuse to add irrelevant details! Provide only the evidence necessary. To do this, consider the audience and how much they need to know. What you say to the CEO of your company about an issue will be different from what you tell your employees. Consider the context of the communication: is this a company-wide email about an organizational change, a private meeting between two people, a presentation to clients, or a presentation at a department meeting?

"Write with a specific person in mind. When writing Berkshire Hathaway's annual report, I pretend that I'm talking to my sisters. I have no trouble picturing them: Though highly intelligent, they are not experts in accounting or finance. They will understand plain English, but jargon may puzzle them. My goal is simply to give them the information I would wish them to supply me if our positions were reversed. To succeed, I don't need to be Shakespeare; I must, though, have a sincere desire to inform. No siblings to write to? Borrow mine: Just begin with 'Dear Doris and Bertie.'"

– Warren Buffett

Warren Buffett is considered one of the most successful investors ever. He's another huge proponent of simplicity in business, communication, and life. Buffett only invests in businesses he understands, he speaks plainly whenever communicating, and he still lives in the house he bought over 50 years ago! How's that for practicing what you preach? Buffett speaks frequently about the need for people to communicate in plain English, particularly when writing and especially in business. What is plain English? It's essentially the English we use in daily life; it's the English I am using to write this book to speak to you. Using plain English in business communication means targeting your audience and using only language they understand. As with the advice above, plain English is not about dumbing things down or omitting important information. It's about simplifying your communication so that your audience understands your message.

Know thy audience: By now, this probably sounds a bit like a broken record, but you must determine your audience. This will affect what is said and how, even when using plain English. Consider your demographics, your familiarity with or understanding of the topic, and what you want from your audience. Are you seeking a sales deal or do you want an employee to start coming into the office on time? Tailor your message to your audience and the context in which they'll receive it.

Ditch the jargon: For your audience to really understand what you mean, it's important to ditch jargon and technical terms and use regular words. This is especially true in communication targeted at clients or customers. You want them to immediately understand what your company or product is all about, particularly when you're advertising online. Your company may know what your service or product is called, but your customers may call it something else. Doing away with jargon is also important in a pitch. If you leave someone scratching her head, she probably won't be jumping to purchase your new service or invest in your company.

Reduce redundancies: Communicating simply and in plain English means not only including the necessary information, but also ensuring you're not repeating information. If someone thinks he's already heard what you've had to say, he isn't as likely to give you his full attention.

Organize, organize, organize: The order in which you discuss ideas is incredibly important when using plain English and for simplicity in your communications. As discussed above, you should lead with the important stuff. Start with the big picture and then discuss the necessary details. Be sure to group related points, which will make your information flow logically and will help to avoid repetition.

Writing tips

Much of what we've already discussed in this chapter is directly applicable to any writing you have to do, but let's go over a few more methods of bringing simplicity and plain English into your written communication.

Use short sentences. Keep your sentences short. Avoid rambling missives and sentences with too many clauses, which are confusing and hard to follow. One way to do this is to use fewer words. That is, don't use multiple words when one will suffice. For example, instead of saying "due to the fact that," simply say "because." Another example is "in order to," which can be changed to just "to" in almost all instances.

Don't write:

In order to carry out a review of the new policy prior to its promulgation, there needs to be a liaison with the addressee no later than January 5.

You can say the same thing with fewer words and enhanced clarity:

To review the new policy before it's issued, we must meet with you by January 5.

Be sure to keep your sections and paragraphs short as well. This will break up the material and make it easier for your audience to take in.

Use verbs. Instead of a noun derived from a verb (these usually end in – tion or –ance), use strong verbs. A strong verb will carry more meaning than a weak verb or a noun, so you'll be able to use fewer words to get your point across.

For example, if you've implemented a new policy that will affect customers, and you want to inform your employees about this, don't write:

We will provide our customers with information about the new policy,

Quickly and simply tell your employees what is happening:

We will inform our customers about the new policy.

Use the active voice. In the active voice, the subject of the sentence performs the action (e.g., the CEO sent the email); in the passive voice, the subject is acted upon (e.g., the email was sent by the CEO). Studies show that people struggle to understand the passive voice. This is because we use the active voice when thinking, which means that when we hear the passive voice, we must take time to mentally convert it to the active. Using the active voice is an easy way to make your writing clear and easy to understand.

If your boss is asking for your monthly report, but you're waiting on a coworker to finish her part, don't say:

A calculation of the figures must be undertaken by Susan before the report can be finished by me.

Simplify your language, use the active voice, and say:

Susan needs to calculate the figures before I can finish the report.

Use examples. When you are writing about something complex or abstract, clarify it for your readers by providing them with examples. Abstract ideas can be made much more understandable when they are used in hypothetical situations that involve people performing actions. So, for example, if you are trying to explain an investment opportunity to a potential client, don't just offer him the numbers and assume that he gets it or will be able to figure it out. Convert the information into a hypothetical situation. Let's look at the excellent example given by A Plain English Handbook for this situation:

For example, you can buy an option from Mr. Smith that gives you the right to buy 100 shares of stock X from him at $25.00 per share anytime between now and six weeks from now. You believe stock X's purchase price will go up between now and then. He believes it will stay the same or go down. If you exercise this option before it expires, Mr. Smith must sell you 100 shares of stock X at $25.00 per share, even if the purchase price has gone up. Either way, whether you exercise your option or not, he keeps the money you paid him for the option.

Using plain language and presenting the information in the form of a hypothetical situation like the example above will help your client quickly understand the opportunity you're offering, which will be less work for you. He also will be more likely to accept an offer he understands.

CONSISTENCY

"Consistently showing up on the radar of the right audience is more highly prized than reaching the masses, once then done."

– Seth Godin

Communicating effectively is only possible when you maintain consistency in any message you deliver, whether this is internally in your company or externally to clients or the media. This may mean that when you are addressing a coworker, you remain consistent in both your verbal and nonverbal messages, or it may mean that you stay consistently "on brand" when selling your product to potential customers. Inconsistent messages are confusing and can lead to discontent and a lack of trust. While the previous chapters were more focused on individual communication in business, this chapter will focus mainly on consistency in corporate communication.

All businesses must have a core message that is delivered clearly and consistently across all platforms. A core message is essentially a picture of what a company is, what it does, and what it can offer customers. Such a message allows employees to work toward a common goal and informs customers and clients of how that company's products or services will benefit them. Without a core message, a company cannot have a defined focus, and consumers won't understand why one company's products are better than those of its competitors.

Companies often have many different brands or products, but the core message or value of a company should be the same. Let's use Apple again as an example: Apple offers a variety of products, from laptops to online music to phones, but its core message is consistent across each product and throughout every channel it uses to communicate. Think of how similar the Apple website is to its physical stores, both with their clean, simple looks and logically divided departments. It doesn't matter if you are buying an iPod online or at the Apple Store, the experience is purposefully designed to be easy and straightforward, much like the products themselves. At its core, Apple's message is simplicity. This core message isn't just for Apple's customers. Apple drives its employees to follow this core value in all their work and in each product. That's a consistent core message, and given Apple's success, it's pretty clear that it works!

A strong core message makes a company memorable and increases consumer trust in the company and its products. Consider Maxwell House, which has been using the slogan "Good to the last drop" since 1917. That slogan is instantly recognizable and is tied to all the products Maxwell House makes. This is not to say that innovation is undesirable, because that's not the case. However, when creating a new product or service, a company should take time to consider whether this is something it should do, especially when that product is considered off-brand. Even while maintaining its nearly 100-year-old slogan, Maxwell House has stayed current and relevant, offering, for example, cups or pods for single-cup coffee makers.

One way a company can ensure it has a consistent core message externally is to make sure that it is communicating consistently across all media platforms, particularly social media. This does not necessarily involve saying the exact same thing on, say, Facebook and Twitter, but the general message should be identical. Your social media posts should stay on topic (i.e., remain within your industry), and you should post in a consistent manner so followers will see your company's name often and can participate actively in the things you are saying. That is what Seth Godin, an American entrepreneur and best-selling author, is getting at in the quote at the beginning of this chapter. You must have the right message, you must get it to the right audience, and you must do both consistently.

It is equally important that this core message is also communicated internally. The core message and values of a company should be clearly and consistently applied across all levels of that company to create and reinforce its culture and vision. Each employee should be familiar with the core message and aim to apply it in everything produced. Think back to Apple—the retail store employee buys in to the core message just as much as the product designers and is as committed to providing the same experience to customers as the designers hope the products themselves provide. This starts by creating a consistent message and consistently communicating it from the very top down.

"You have to have an authentic voice . . . A consistent, authentic voice, which is you."

– Tim Ferriss

The element of consistency can and should be applied to the individual level of communication. When you are consistent in the way you communicate with others in the workplace, you can benefit in the same way a company benefits from a consistent core message—you'll be seen as trustworthy, knowledgeable, and valuable. But if you're all over the place in your communications and reactions to others, people will be wary of you and will be less motivated to do things that benefit you, like promote you to another position, approach you with ideas, or any number of things that would increase your success in the workplace. Being consistent in your communication with your coworkers and employees also makes the daily running of the business much smoother and less chaotic.

According to the American Management Association's Global Study of Current Trends and Future Possibilities 2007-2017, "an organization's consistency of strategic approach helps determine its success. This consistency can be measured to see how well the organization 'walks the talk.' High-performance organizations tend to establish clear visions that are supported by flexible and achievable strategic plans. They also have clearly articulated philosophies that set the standards for everyone's behavior. In addition, they have leaders, managers, and employees who behave consistently with the strategic plan and the company's philosophy." The study goes on to say that when leaders tell employees they should behave one way and then are inconsistent themselves, employees may believe the leaders do not actually believe in what they say. Employees may even come to believe that the rules do not apply to everyone and they can do whatever they'd like. This is not a recipe for success!

Communicating consistently will help you get the results you want. Think about it this way: If you're trying to get your employees to be more candid with you, as we discussed earlier, and one day you are open to such feedback but the next day you're angry about it, your inconsistent behavior will put people off. They will not feel secure in giving you the feedback you want. When you are inconsistent in how you communicate, you confuse those receiving your messages. However, when you are consistent and follow through on what you say, you are perceived as reliable and credible, and you will be respected. You can only expect to both achieve and receive consistent results if you yourself are consistent.

You can bring consistency to your daily workplace communication in the following ways:

Thorough understanding. To have a consistent and tight focus, you must really understand what it is you are communicating, so know your stuff from top to bottom. When you aren't sure what you are talking about, you are much more likely to give inconsistent messages.

Stay on point. A clear and consistent message demands you stay on topic. Avoid telling rambling stories or anecdotes, especially ones that are only loosely tied to your main idea.

Follow through. When you say you will do something, be sure to actually do it. This sounds simple, but lack of follow through is one of the biggest frustrations in the workplace.

Match yourself. Be sure that what you say matches what you do. Your words, body language, and tone of voice must match to be seen as consistent. If you are telling your employees you want a workplace that is respectful, but you are seen deriding someone, it will be hard for your employees to believe you mean what you say.

Be fair. You should treat your employees or coworkers equally and fairly. Of course, it is human nature to have closer relationships with certain people over others, but be sure you are consistently treating people equally in the workplace. Using the desire for feedback as our example again, don't accept feedback only from favored staff and balk when it comes from someone else.

Open expectations. Be open and clear about your expectations and repeat them when necessary. It is confusing and frustrating for your employees when your expectations aren't being clearly expressed or when you seem to change them every day.

Writing tips

Of all the factors of successful communication that we've discussed, consistency is probably the easiest to apply to your writing. Here are a few helpful pointers to get you started:

Maintain your voice. A voice that varies across a document is probably the most common way inconsistency sneaks into writing. Ensure you are using the same tone and voice throughout any document you are writing. If you are writing a formal proposal, make sure to maintain a formal tone and avoid using informal language. Watch for the inconsistent use of terms—if you use a particular name or phrase for something, use it consistently throughout, or your readers may think you are talking about different things.

This is also something to watch for if multiple people are working on a document. One way to ensure a consistent voice across such documents is to have one person edit the final document. Plus, doing so will get rid of all the little errors that sneak into writing.

The little things. It may seem unimportant, but be consistent in things like formatting, capitalization, font types, punctuation, the treatment of numbers, and so on. It is frustrating and distracting to read a document in which the author is all over the place with these little things, and it can even seem as if the writer was lazy or didn't care.

Consider what you would think if you received a proposal with the following sentences:

A&b Inc is the leading document management company. With offices in over 9 countries and seven customizable product solutions, I'm confident that A and B Inc. can meet all your document management needs.

The inconsistencies look sloppy and unprofessional, and they certainly don't engender confidence in the company or its products.

Grammar counts. Watch for things like tense or parallel construction, as these are areas where even the best writers are sometimes inconsistent. Such mistakes can be confusing for your readers. If you are writing in the present tense, be careful not to slip into past tense. To use parallel structure correctly, remember that items in a list must be in the same grammatical form.

For example, it is incorrect to say the following when asking an employee to do something for you:

I need you to write the report, the email, and call the client.

To make the structure parallel, you must say:

I need you to write the report and the email and call the client.

A cleanly written document will always be better received than one full of inconsistencies and grammar errors, enhancing both your communication and your business success.

CONCLUSION

"The single biggest problem in communication is the illusion that it has taken place."

– George Bernard Shaw

George Bernard Shaw, playwright and founder of the London School of Economics, is right—the biggest problem we have when communicating is the belief that we're doing it well or at all. Hopefully, now that we've reached the end of this book, you have an appreciation of the importance of communication and have a better idea of areas in which you can improve, as well as how to do so.

Effective communication may be the most important aspect of a business's success, and this is true for you personally, whether you are the CEO or an entry-level employee. In the introduction, we talked about communication failures and their outcomes, but what happens when a business is communicating effectively, both internally and externally? What happens to such a business is that it succeeds, and in very measureable ways. The "Effective Communication: A Leading Indicator of Financial Performance - 2005/2006 Communication ROI Study" found that companies that communicate effectively have a market premium that is 19.4% higher than companies that do not; in fact, companies that communicate ineffectively actually experience a 15% decrease in market valuation. Shareholder returns for companies communicating effectively are more than 57% higher than for companies that do not. It's not just monetary gains that come from increased effective communication: Organizations that communicate well have employee engagement levels that are 4.5 times higher than organizations that communicate less effectively, and such companies are 20% more likely to report lower turnover rates. Effective communication also leads to higher rates of productivity among employees.

It's hard to argue with numbers like those!

As an individual, you can use the tips and tools in this book to improve your communication immediately and in your everyday work. In doing so, you will see your working relationships improve, your productivity and output will increase, and you'll be more successful in your work overall. Of course, part of communicating effectively is also about finding what works best for you while you are putting what we've discussed into practice. Mark Zuckerberg, one of the co-founders of Facebook, is known for taking people on walks in the woods near his company's headquarters when he wants to talk to them about something serious, particularly when pitching to them. Steve Jobs was also said to have gone for walks when wanting to discuss his thoughts.

If you're a leader or manager, one further step you may want to take to ensure that your organization is communicating as well as possible is to create a communication plan, so let's go over that as one final way to increase your communication success.

A communication plan determines the market your company is trying to target, as well as when, how, and with what message. It guides your company's external communication, ensuring that the right message is sent to the right audience, from the right person, through the correct channel, and at the right time. This in turn creates a foundation on which to make decisions and come up with ideas to focus your organization on the right things. You can put together a communication plan by following these five easy steps:

1. Define your goals and objectives. You must first determine your goals, which are your long-term aims, and then identify your objectives, which are the short-term steps that will help you reach those goals.

2. Define your target audience. Before you can figure out what message to send and how to send it, you must first determine to whom you want to send it. Who are you trying to reach? Who are your customers? Try to be specific here.

3. Define your key message. This is where you decide what you want your audience to hear. What do you want your customers to know about your product or service?

4. Create a strategy. In this step, choose the appropriate vehicles for your message and determine the resources you'll need to send your message. At this point, you also identify the changes that need to be made to how you currently communicate, and then you create a plan for implementing these changes.

5. Evaluate. After implementing your communication plan, you need to evaluate it to determine whether you are meeting your objectives. Adjust your goals, objectives, and strategies as necessary.

The key here is that once you have created a communication plan, you must actually communicate it! In a survey by International Survey Research, a Chicago-based research and consulting firm, 63% of the employees surveyed stated that they find out about important work news through gossip, not from their managers. This kind of communication is often inaccurate, which could lead to discord or panic, depending on what is being spread around (e.g., hearing that big changes to the company are in the works may cause employees to fear for their jobs), and can make employees feel unvalued and unmotivated. Be sure that you are communicating the new plan across your company and make sure that employees are not only aware of the plan, but also committed to it.

That's it! We've reached the end of this quick guide to communication. There is so much more to say about this one, seemingly simple thing that we spend most of our lives doing. However, if there is only one thing you take away from all that we've discussed, make it this: Know your audience. If you understand with whom you're communicating, much of the rest will follow.

Acknowledgments and Works Cited

All references within this text are fully acknowledged and, where possible, linked directly to the source material. We now offer two alphabetical lists of all references and works cited within the body of this guide. The first list consists of online resources and the second refers to those in print.

Online references

The Blog of Tim Ferriss

How to Write and Promote New York Times Bestsellers: Tim Ferriss and Jack Canfield

http://www.fourhourworkweek.com/blog/2012/09/01/how-to-write-and-promote-new-york-times-bestsellers-tim-ferriss-and-jack-canfield/

British Council

Business Writing Lessons

http://www.britishcouncil.org/professionals-lesson-downloads-business-writing-homepage.htm

BusinessWeek

RIM's BlackBerry: Failure to Communicate

http://www.businessweek.com/magazine/content/10_42/b4199076785733.htm

Steve Jobs: "There's Sanity Returning"

http://www.businessweek.com/1998/21/b3579165.htm

Business Insider

When Mark Zuckerberg Really Wants to Hire You, He'll Ask You to Take a Walk with Him in the Woods http://www.businessinsider.com/mark-zuckerberg-walk-in-the-woods-2011-7

Carrie Hannigan

Facilitating Gossip in the Workplace

http://www.carriehannigan.com/gossip.html

Center for Appropriate Dispute Resolution in Special Education

Communication Skills

http://www.directionservice.org/cadre/

CNN

Cartoon Network Boss Quits Over Bomb Scare

http://money.cnn.com/2007/02/09/news/newsmakers/cartoon_network/

Two Held after Ad Campaign Triggers Boston Bomb Scare

http://www.cnn.com/2007/US/01/31/boston.bombscare/

Daily Mail

Billionaire Warren Buffet Still Lives in Modest Omaha Home He Bought For $31,500 in 1958 (Though He Does Have $4m Californian Home - But Even That Was a Bargain)

http://www.dailymail.co.uk/news/article-2265703/Warren-Buffet-lives-modest-Omaha-home-bought-31-500-1958.html

Divine Caroline

Speak Up! How to Be Assertive At Work

http://www.divinecaroline.com/life-etc/career-money/speak-how-be-assertive-work

Forbes

How to Communicate Effectively at Work

http://www.forbes.com/sites/susanadams/2011/11/21/how-to-communicate-effectively-at-work/

Ten Tips for Better Business Writing

http://www.forbes.com/pictures/emig45gmmh/10-tips-for-better-business-writing/

Georgia State University

How to Build a High-Performance Organization: A Global Study of Current Trends and Future Possibilities 2007-2017

http://www.studymode.com/essays/How-To-Build-a-High-Performance-Organization-1673631.html

The Globe and Mail

With HP Tablet Dead, Who Can Challenge Apple?

http://www.theglobeandmail.com/technology/tech-news/with-hp-tablet-dead-who-can-challenge-apple/article592378/

The Guardian

The Secret of Apple's Success: Simplicity

http://www.theguardian.com/money/2012/jun/15/secret-apple-success-simplicity

Harvard Business Review

The Real Leadership Lessons of Steve Jobs

http://hbr.org/2012/04/the-real-leadership-lessons-of-steve-jobs/

Stay on Message to Win Buy-In

http://blogs.hbr.org/2011/01/stay-on-message-to-win-buy-in/

Huffington Post

Gulf Oil Spill Timeline and the Ensuing Legal Cases Against BP

http://www.huffingtonpost.com/2012/11/15/gulf-oil-spill-timeline_n_2139515.html

Sheryl Sandberg: A New Metaphor for Your Career

http://www.huffingtonpost.com/sheryl-sandberg/class-day-speech_b_1557898.html

Inc.

A Crash Course in Communication

http://www.inc.com/articles/2000/08/20000.html

10 Smart Rules for Giving Negative Feedback

http://www.inc.com/articles/2000/08/20000.html

Interpersonal Project Management Communications

Consistency of Message in Communicating to Your Team

http://intpmcomms.com/consistency-of-message-in-communicating-to-your-team/

Jamillah Warner

A Simple Thing That Apple Knows About Marketing Communication That You Don't!

http://www.jamillahwarner.com/marketing-communication-lessons-from-apple/

Lucid Lingo

How to Write Copy like Warren Buffett

http://www.lucidlingo.com.au/blog/how-to-write-copy-like-warren-buffett/

Mark Evans Tech

Without Core Messaging, You're DOA

http://www.markevanstech.com/tag/core-messaging/

Marketing Trenches

Who Are You? The 5 Key Components of a Core Messaging Document

http://www.marketingtrenches.com/marketing-strategy/who-are-you-the-5-key-components-of-a-core-messaging-document/

Mayo Clinic

Being Assertive: Reduce Stress, Communication Better

http://www.mayoclinic.com/health/assertive/SR00042

MTD

How to Get Honest Feedback from Your Employees

http://www.m-t-d.co.uk/blog/how-to-get-honest-feedback-from-your-employees.htm

Mulhauser Consulting, Ltd.

Listening, Understanding and Business Empathy

http://mulhauser.net/lib/business/coaching-mentoring/listening/

NBC News

Oil Spill Investigators Focus on Communication

http://www.nbcnews.com/id/38818600/

NewSchools Venture Fund

Innovation and Entrepreneurship in Education

http://blog.citigroup.com/2012/09/innovation-and-entrepreneurship-in-education.shtml

New York Times

No Ranting and Raving Is Permitted

http://www.nytimes.com/2011/11/13/business/robert-l-johnson-anger-has-no-place-in-business.html?pagewanted=all&_r=0

NSC Blog

Written Communication Skills: The Importance of Simplicity

http://www.nscblog.com/miscellaneous/written-communication-skills-the-importance-of-simplicity/

Ontario Ministry of Agriculture and Food

Communication Planning for Organizations

http://www.omafra.gov.on.ca/english/rural/facts/03-033.htm

PlainLanguage.gov

http://www.plainlanguage.gov/

Purdue OWL

Workplace Writers

https://owl.english.purdue.edu/owl/resource/681/01/

Psychology Today

The Most Dangerous Word in the World

http://www.psychologytoday.com/blog/words-can-change-your-brain/201207/the-most-dangerous-word-in-the-world

RT Design Group

Consistency in Social Media Communication

http://www.rtdesigngroup.com/blog/consistency-in-social-media-communication.html

Science Daily

Many English Speakers Cannot Understand Basic Grammar

http://www.sciencedaily.com/releases/2010/07/100706082156.htm

Seth Godin's Blog

Volatility and Value

http://sethgodin.typepad.com/seths_blog/2012/05/volatility-and-value.html

Smithsonian.com

How Steve Jobs' Love of Simplicity Fueled a Design Revolution

http://www.smithsonianmag.com/arts-culture/How-Steve-Jobs-Love-of-Simplicity-Fueled-A-Design-Revolution-166251016.html

Solari

The Most Successful Companies Communication Better

http://www.solari.net/documents/position-papers/Solari-The-Most-Successful-Companies-Communicate-Better.pdf

Steven R Covey

Habit 5: Seek First to Understand, Then To Be Understood

https://www.stephencovey.com/7habits/7habits-habit5.php

TMCnet

The Top Five Reasons Communications Fail

https://www.stephencovey.com/7habits/7habits-habit5.php

University of Kent

Communication Skills

http://www.kent.ac.uk/careers/sk/communicating.htm

University of Maine

Effective Communication

http://www.umext.maine.edu/onlinepubs/pdfpubs/6103.pdf

U.S. Securities and Exchange Commission

A Plain English Handbook

http://www.sec.gov/pdf/handbook.pdf

Watson Wyatt

2009/2010 Communication ROI Study

http://www.watsonwyatt.com/research/pdfs/WT_2009_13506.pdf

Research Report

http://www.watsonwyatt.com/research/reports.asp

Wikipedia

2007 Boston Bomb Scare

http://en.wikipedia.org/wiki/2007_Boston_bomb_scare

KISS Principle

http://en.wikipedia.org/wiki/KISS_principle

Maxwell House

http://en.wikipedia.org/wiki/Maxwell_House

Wired

Live Coverage: Apple's Special Tablet Event

http://www.wired.com/gadgetlab/2010/01/apple-tablet-event/

Wisconsin School of Business

Practicing Candor

http://bus.wisc.edu/~/media/exed/courses/leadership%20beyond%20management/leadingyourmanager.ashx

Yale University

HR Communicator's Toolkit

http://www.yale.edu/hronline/communications/hr_communicators_toolkit.html

Print references

Becker, Ethan F., and Jon Wortmann. *Mastering Communication at Work: How to Lead, Manage, and Influence*. New York: McGraw Hill, 2009.

Brounstein, Marty. *Communicating Effectively for Dummies*. New York: Wiley Publishing Inc., 2001.

Buffett, Mary, and David Clark. *Warren Buffett's Management Secrets*. New York: Simon & Schuster Inc., 2009.

Carnegie, Dale. *How to Win Friends and Influence People*. New York: Simon & Schuster Inc., 1998.

Covey, Stephen R. *The Seven Habits of Highly Effective People*. New York: RosettaBooks LLC, 2012.

Dickinson, Arlene. *Persuasion: A New Approach to Changing Minds.* Toronto: HarperCollins Publishers Ltd., 2011.

Ferriss, Tim. *The 4-Hour Workweek: Escape 9–5, Live Anywhere, and Join the New Rich.* New York: Random House Inc., 2009.

Sander, Peter. *What Would Steve Jobs Do?* New York: McGraw Hill, 2012.

Taylor, Shirley, and Alison Lester. *Communication: Your Key to Success*. Singapore: Marshall Cavendish Business, 2009.

Welch, Jack, and Suzy Welch. *Winning*. New York: HarperCollins Publishers Ltd., 2005.

ABOUT THE AUTHOR

Scribendi.com was founded in 1997 as one of the world's first online editing and proofreading companies. Based in Ontario, Canada, the company's primary goal is to provide clients with fast, reliable, and affordable revision services. Today, Scribendi.com is the world's largest online proofreading and editing company.